SunShyne- Direct light of the sun. Brightness or radiance; cheerfulness or happiness. Also means captain, good, and graceful.

SunShyne began her walk to school and along the way she constantly had to remind herself that everything was going to be okay. She passed by the park that her and Alisha always bring Athena to when she wants to go for a walk. SunShyne thought about the time Athena almost got away from them because she was trying to chase birds. The very thought of Athena's tiny legs scurrying along that day made SunShyne laugh out loud. She turned around quickly to see if anyone had heard her laughter. But she realized that she was the only who heard the laughter.

Have you ever thought about something in your mind that made you laugh out loud?

When SunShyne realized nobody else was around she started talking to herself out loud to give herself some encouragement. "Ok SunShyne, you got this! Everything will be fine, everything will be fine!". She repeated and then took a couple of deep breaths and continued walking down the street until her school appeared before her. SunShyne stood still on the sidewalk as she watched the cars drive by, she even watched as a group of students got off of the school bus in front of the school. SunShyne stood on the sidewalk until traffic came to a pause, she made sure she was in the crosswalk before making her way across the street to her school.

What should you do first before trying to cross the street?

SunShyne made her way across the street safely and then began walking up the stairs towards the front door of the school building. Her heart started pounding really hard and fast. SunShyne also felt the palms of her hands getting sweaty followed by a feeling of warmth all over her body so she stood there for a moment. Finally she places her right hand on the handle of the door and took a few more deep breaths before she pulled the door open. As soon as she opened the door the noise grew louder and louder making SunShyne even more nervous.

What is the name of your school? What grade are you currently in?

When SunShyne finally made her way through the entrance she seen a bunch of people in the main hallway. The students were yelling really loud trying to talk over one another, some were running around, and even bouncing balls in the hallway and it was complete chaos. There were two teachers who kept trying to get the chaos under control but it was just too late! SunShyne already felt overwhelmed, so she ran into the closest bathroom she could find. SunShyne, pushed the door opened as fast as she could and with tears bouncing off of her cheeks she ran towards the sink.

Do you remember your first day of school?

SunShyne turned on the water, and looked in the mirror. She saw the tears flowing rapidly down her cheeks and just stood there for a moment.

"Ok, you have to get yourself together! You got this" SunShyne repeated to herself. She tried to smile but she just couldn't the tears kept flowing. She stood there trying to figure out why she was so upset and afraid of crowds and loud noises. Nobody else in her family seems to be bothered by it the way that she is so SunShyne cried even more because she didn't understand why she was different from everyone else in her family. She leaned over the sink and slashed water on her face and as soon as she wiped the water out of her eyes and reached for a paper towel she heard the bathroom door open.

Do loud noises and crowds make you nervous?

"Hello!" SunShyne heard a soft voice say. Then she heard the voice again "Are you ok? I saw you run in here in a hurry so I wanted to come in and check on you. My name is Ayana". SunShyne didn't turn around to see who was speaking instead she kept her head down as she tore a piece of paper towel from the dispenser. SunShyne tried her hardest to stop her tears from flowing before she spoke "My name is SunShyne she said in a mellow tone. I'm ok, its my first day here and seeing all of those kids in the hall made me really nervous." Ayana walked over to SunShyne and put her hand on her shoulder. "It's ok I know how you feel. I was very nervous on my first day of school too".

Ayana continued to try to comfort SunShyne "Oh yeah SunShyne, I understand that feeling! My last school wasn't this big either, but after a while you'll get used to it. When I first started here I felt so lost and scared because I didn't know anyone. I have always gone to school with my cousins and siblings but now I am all on my own. It was hard at first but it has allowed me to grow in so many ways. I feel so independent now! Don't worry SunShyne, I got your back. I'm not sure if we have the same classes but I will be sure to look out for you in the cafeteria".

Have you ever hid to avoid doing something?

SunShyne turned towards Ayana and spoke "Thank you, Ayana! That makes me feel a little better. I'm sorry we had to meet like this! But for as long as I can remember I have always been afraid of being in a room full of people or in crowds especially when its really noisy. It's usually not too bad when there are only a few people. Its a big different when I'm around people I really know. School has always been very difficult for me because there are always a lot of people around, not to mention I had a dream last night that probably didn't help". Ayana looked at SunShyne with suspense.

"What kind of dream?" Ayana asked. SunShyne explained "in my dream people made fun of my name, I couldn't find any of my classes, and the biggest thing was tripping in the cafeteria in front of everyone"! "Wow, SunShyne that is horrible! I don't think any of those things will happen especially if I can help it" Ayana said. "Thank you, Ayana". "You're welcome SunShyne, now lets get out of here before the bell rings and we are late". SunShyne smiled and nodded her head, then they both headed towards the bathroom door. Before they reached the door SunShyne stopped to make sure she didn't look like she had been crying.

What would you tell SunShyne to help her feel better?

Ayana placed her hand on the door knob but before Ayana could open it, the door swung open and it was none other than Reyna, the last person who Ayana wanted to see. "Well, well what do we have here"? Reyna asked with a smirk on her face. "Reyna! You almost hit me with the door"! Ayana exclaimed. "Oh relax, Ayana it didn't hit you so no need to cry about it, you big baby!" Reyna replied. SunShyne just stood quietly trying really hard not to make eye contact with Reyna, but Reyna did everything in her power to get SunShyne's attention. Reyna continued to stare at SunShyne.

"Hey! Are you new? I haven't seen you around here before" Reyna said . "Reyna, she doesn't have to tell you anything! Minding your own business is so important" said Ayana as she rolled her eyes at Reyna. Ayana turned towards SunShyne, "You don't have to answer her! She is always in somebody's business and think she runs the school because she is popular and good at everything, except for minding her own business." Ayana said with a laugh. SunShyne couldn't help but chuckle which really made Reyna mad, so she stormed by Ayana and SunShyne and made her way into a bathroom stall. Both of the girls laughed and headed out of the bathroom.

How do you think SunShyne and Ayana handled the situation with Reyna? What would you have done in this situation?

As SunShyne and Ayana made their way out of the bathroom and down the hall into Ms. Ruben's class the bell rung, and they both sighed a breath of relief because they had barely beat the tardy bell. Ms. Ruben was standing by the door and greeted the girls as they walked in. "You must be SunShyne! Nice to meet you" said Ms. Ruben. SunShyne spoke softly "Thank you, nice to meet you too". While standing in the door way SunShyne's eyes quickly scanned the room where she saw about twenty other students sitting in their seats. SunShyne was so surprised to see so many students in one class because at her old school there was a total of twelve students in each class.

SunShyne glanced around the room again until she spotted an empty seat towards the back of the classroom. She made her way towards the back as all the other students watched her as she walked by. "Excuse me" SunShyne said softly as she stepped over the feet of her classmates. Ms. Ruben tapped her pointer against the wall to get the attention of the students "Class let's clear the way so that our new student can get to her seat!" Ms. Ruben said loudly. The students cleared the way for SunShyne as she walked by to get to her seat. Her heart was pounding as she slid her chair back and sat down in her seat.

How many students are in your class?

After SunShyne took her seat she heard whispering and laughter from behind her but she was too afraid to turn around and see who it was. The laughter continued and SunShyne finally found the courage to turn around to see who it was. "Justin!" Ms. Ruben said with a stern look on her face, "sit down and be quiet!" As the rumble of Ms. Ruben's voice filled the room all of the students fell silent and looked straight ahead including SunShyne. She was happy that Ms. Ruben had stopped the teasing that was going on behind her back.

"Okay everyone, now that I have gotten your attention I'd like to take this time to welcome our new student to our class!" Ms. Ruben said with a smile. All the students turned towards SunShyne. "Welcome" a few voices said, while a few others repeated her name. "SunShyne! wow what a cool name" she overheard one student say. SunShyne sat back with a smile on her face, she took her notebook out of her backpack and placed it on her desk. "SunShyne, would you like to come up and tell us a little about yourself?" Ms. Ruben said while waving her hands excitedly inviting SunShyne to the front of the classroom.

SunShyne nervously walked up to the front of the class and stood there silently as her classmates anxiously starred at her. She gave a half smile and began to speak softly. "Um as you know I am new here, we just moved here a week ago. My dad got a new job so we moved here". Ms. Ruben could tell SunShyne was uncomfortable because she noticed that SunShyne was tapping her hands on the side of legs, she also avoided making eye contact with her classmates, and appeared to be breaking out in a sweat. Ms. Ruben walked over to SunShyne and stood beside her in hopes to give her some comfort as she spoke.

How do you feel when your teacher call on you to speak in class?

SunShyne continued "I have a 6 month old yorkie named Athena we go on walks every day and sometimes she even likes to chase birds in the park". The class filled with laughter and the laughter made SunShyne feel a little less nervous. "I have two sisters who are super cool, and my mom makes delicious treats!, well I guess that's it". The erupted in applause. SunShyne smiled as she realized she had faced one of her biggest fears which was speaking in front of people. Ayana jumped up and cheered "Yay SunShyne!" It took a lot for SunShyne to stand up in front of the class and speak so Ayana wanted to make sure she celebrated SunShyne.

Do you celebrate when your friends do well?

As SunShyne walked back to her seat she thought about how proud her family would have been to see her standing up in front of her class being brave enough to speak. SunShyne was also very proud of herself because although she was nervous she did not allow her nervousness to stop her, instead she worked through it and got it done! By the time Ms. Ruben got done going over the new reading assignment class was coming to an end. The bell rung, all of the students jumped up, grabbed their belongings and headed towards the door. SunShyne pulled her schedule out to see which class she had next, then she walked over to Ms. Ruben and asked for directions on how to get to her math class.

SunShyne walked up the long staircase and made her way towards her math class which was taught by Mr. Johnson.

When she arrived she noticed that the classroom was empty. SunShyne was confused and wondered where everyone was. She took out her schedule again to make sure she was in the right classroom. As SunShyne is looking down at her schedule she hears a voice behind her. "Excuse me"! SunShyne turned around to see who was behind her. She noticed a tall man wearing glasses standing on the stairs. She turned back around and looked at the empty classroom. "Where is everyone? Am I in the right class?" SunShyne started to feel like her dream was coming true. She stood still and then she heard the voice again "Excuse me"!

SunShyne turned back around towards the the staircase. "I'm sorry its just that my schedule says I am supposed to be in this class for math, but nobody is here." SunShyne said as she held up her schedule. "Oh yes! You must be the new student. Hi, I'm Mr. Johnson your math teacher. My apologies, on Mondays we usually meet in the media center which is upstairs". SunShyne exhaled with relief "For a second I thought I was in the wrong class" she said with a nervous chuckle. "Please forgive me, I completely forgot that you were starting today until I got the class settled and took attendance, then I realized there was a good chance you were down here".

Have you ever walked into the wrong class?

SunShyne was so relieved that her dream had not come true. She followed Mr. Johnson up the stairs, down the hall, and through the double doors that led to the media center. Once inside SunShyne noticed a few familiar faces from Ms. Ruben's class and before she could finish scanning the room Ayana waved her over to her table. "Hey SunShyne I didn't know we were in the same math until Mr. Johnson called your name for attendance, had I known we could have walked here together". SunShyne nodded her head and then sat down in the seat next to Ayana.

Mr. Johnson stood guard as the students worked on their assignments. SunShyne silently struggled with her math assignment because she tried several times to get Mr. Johnson's attention to ask for help, but he repeatedly told her to be quiet; so SunShyne tried her best because that's what her mother always told her to do. Once SunShyne was done with her assignment she closed her laptop and sat quietly until the rest of the students finished their assignments. When all of the students were done Mr. Johnson gave them free time to do whatever they wanted to so SunShyne and Ayana decided to play games on their laptops until the bell rung to head to lunch.

What time do you eat lunch at school?

As SunShyne entered the cafeteria she noticed a long line of students none of who she recognized. After grabbing her lunch tray SunShyne walked over to an empty table and sat down to eat her lunch alone, but that didn't last long! Justin, Ayana, Reyna, and Eric all sat down at the table with SunShyne. SunShyne smiled but tried to hide the overwhelming excitement she was feeling on the inside. She was so happy that she didn't have to eat lunch alone. The students shared stories about themselves and by the end of lunch SunShyne felt like she was part of the "crew", well that was until Justin started making fun her struggling with the math assignment. Thankfully Eric came to her rescue.

SunShyne smiled and thanked Eric for speaking up for her. They all finished up their lunch and threw their garbage away then heading out of the cafeteria. Eric and Ayana walked to Science class together, while Reyna walked in the opposite direction heading to Art class leaving Justin and SunShyne to walk together to gym class. Justin playfully tapped every locker along the way, trying his hardest to get on SunShyne's nerve but she ignored his attempt. When Justin realized that SunShyne wasn't bothered by his behavior he stopped. As they continued walking SunShyne could feel Justin looking at her so she turned towards him.

Have you ever had someone make fun of you? How did it make you feel?

Justin noticed that SunShyne had stopped walking and was starring back at him. "What are you looking at?" Justin yelled. "You!" SunShyne replied with a firm tone. Justin was shocked by the tone of SunShyne's voice, she had been very soft spoken the entire day and now her voice echoed through the hall. Justin could see that he finally succeeded at upsetting SunShyne so he laughed "Ha ha ha! Are you going to cry? You look like you want to cry!". No matter how hard Justin laughed SunShyne never took her eyes off of him, "Justin, why are you being a bully?" she asked. "I'm not being a bully I'm just having fun" Justin replied. "Well this isn't fun for me." said SunShyne.

Justin's smile went away "Geesh SunShyne lighten up a bit I was only playing! Don't be so sensitive". SunShyne knew that she was not just being sensitive, she knew that Justin was going out of his way to bother her but she wasn't going to take it. SunShyne decided to stick up for herself "Justin, you may think it is funny to make fun of people or do annoying thing to try to be funny but it isn't. I have always had a hard time doing math and completing my assignments on time, so while you may think it's funny it isn't funny to me. Can you please stop!"? Justin laughed then stepped in front of SunShyne as they entered the gym almost causing her to fall.

Mr. Malone blew his whistle to get the student's attention. Mr. Malone is the gym teacher as well as the school's basketball coach. Once the students heard the sound of the whistle they stopped talking and looked at Mr. Malone who gave them instructions on how to do their basketball drills. Each student took turns throwing the basketball from the free-throw line and when they were done Mr. Malone had them run laps around the gym. Justin led the way running way ahead of the class "I'm the fastest in the class nobody can beat me in a race!". Mr. Malone blew his whistle and all of the students stopped running .

What is your favorite thing to do in gym class?

Mr. Malone told all of the students to line up against the wall, "Okay everyone it seems as though we have a showoff on our hands. It appears that Mr. Justin here, feels as though he is the fastest in the class and that nobody can beat him in a race so is there anyone here who would like to challenge his theory?". All of the students looked around at each other but none of them said anything so Mr. Malone told Justin to stand on the white line under the basketball hoop. Justin walked over and stood on the line. Mr. Malone handed his whistle to SunShyne and then walked over and stood beside Justin. Justin realized that Mr. Malone had accepted his challenge.

The students cheered as they watched Mr. Malone's foot cross the orange cones before Justin. All of the students cheered and celebrated, they even jumped up and down in excitement. Mr. Malone taught Justin and important lesson by beating him. After the race Justin apologized for his behavior and then walked over to SunShyne, "Look SunShyne I'm sorry about earlier. I didn't mean to hurt your feelings I was just trying to have a little fun, sometimes I can get carried away but I don't want to hurt anyone". SunShyne accepted Justin's apology and offered him a cup of cold water because he was sweating from all of the running.

Have you ever accepted an apology from someone who has hurt your feelings?

After the students cleaned themselves up they helped Mr. Malone clean up the gym, since they were his last class of the day. Mr. Malone thanked them and told the students that they earned fifteen minutes of free time next class for helping him. Once all of the equipment was back in the closet the bell rung and it was time for everyone to go to their final class of the day. SunShyne pulled out her schedule and noticed that her last class was Science. As she was walking down the hall she heard her name being called "SunShyne! SunShyne! wait up". SunShyne turned around to see Eric quickly walking down the hall to catch up to her.

SunShyne waited for Eric to catch up to her and then they both looked at her schedule and he walked her to her class, "SunShyne I hope you have enjoyed your first day of school. I know Justin can be a real pain but once you get to know him he isn't that bad". SunShyne smiled and nodded her head. She told Eric about what happened in gym class. Eric laughed at Justin getting beat in a race because he knew that Justin thought he was the fastest person in the world. SunShyne admitted to Eric that she didn't think Justin was a bad person anymore because he had apologized to her in front of the entire gym class.

Do you think you can win a race?

After the last bell of the day rung SunShyne grabbed her backpack and made her way through the crowded halls and down the stairs towards the front door. She was so excited to get home and tell her family about the all the things that happened on her first day of school. SunShyne walked down the street with a huge smile on her face. Once she got home Athena ran towards her and greeted her with lots of licks! SunShyne's mother had made her some delicious treats to eat while doing her homework. SunShyne told Tweetie and Alisha all about Justin, Reyna, Eric, and Ayana! She was so excited to have met friends on her first day of school.

Written by Author SunShyne B

Made in the USA
Columbia, SC
12 January 2024